ISBN: 978-1517614836

Created by Native Child Dinétah, Flagstaff, AZ 86003

www.nativechild.com   info@nativechild.com
www.facebook.com/dinetah

by J.B. Enochs

illustrated by Gerald Nailor

Design, Layout and Cover Art by Bernhard Michaelis

Colorization of Cover by Dalasie Michaelis

Little Man's Family

Diné Yázhí Ba'áłchíní

Reader Coloring Book

by

J.B. Enochs

illustrated by

Gerald Nailor

This **Coloring Book**
is a companion to Little Man's Family **Reader**

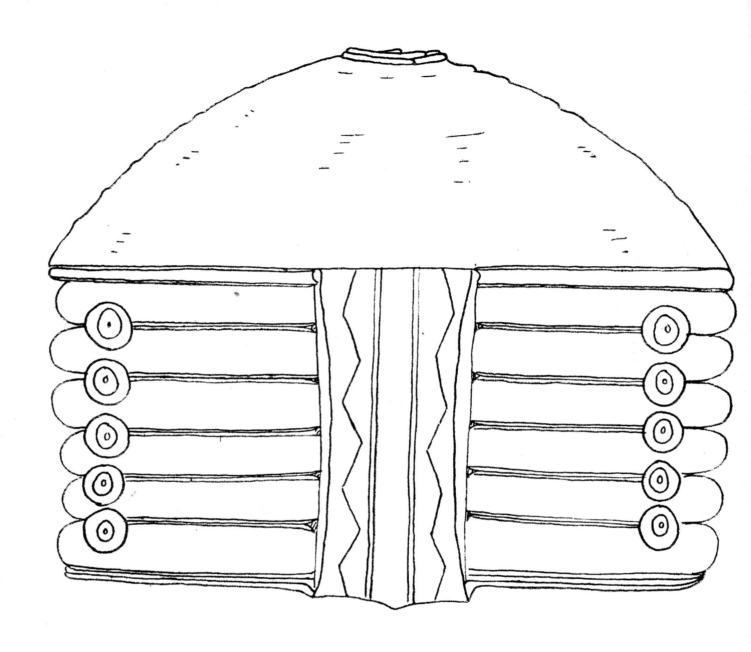

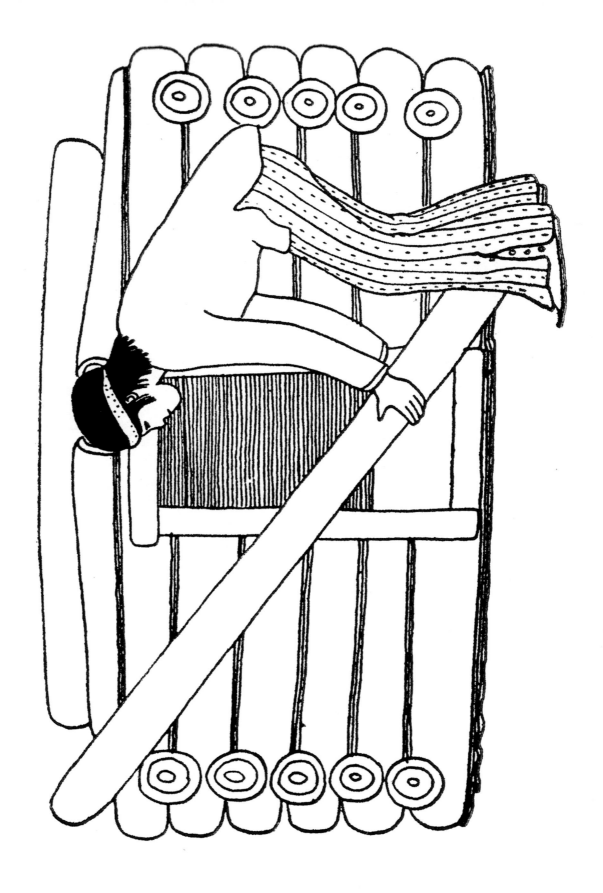

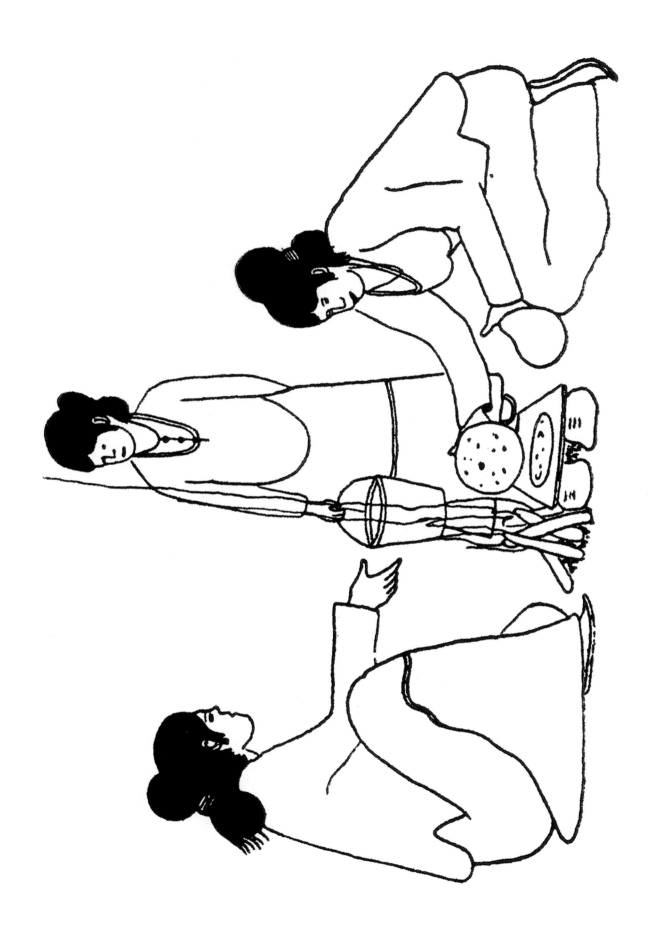

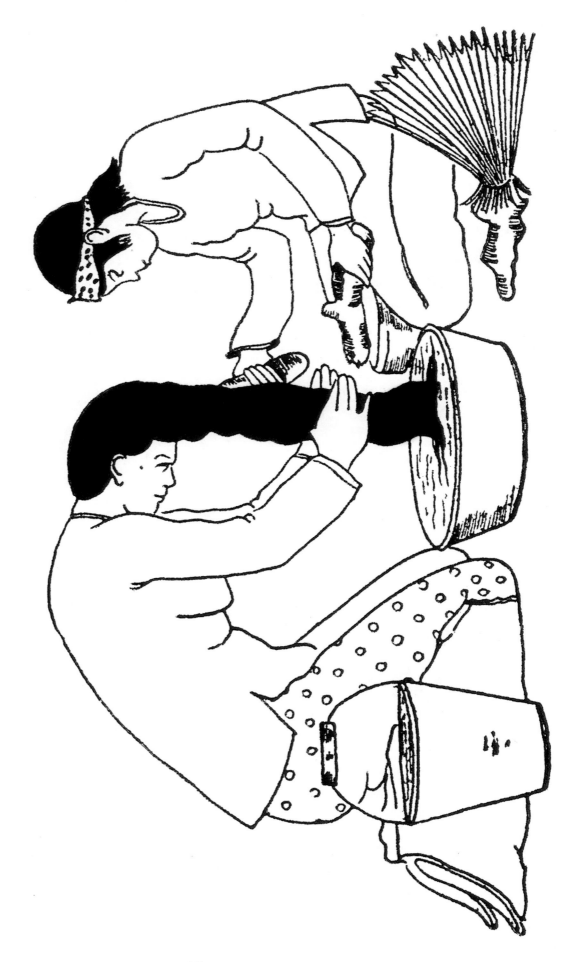

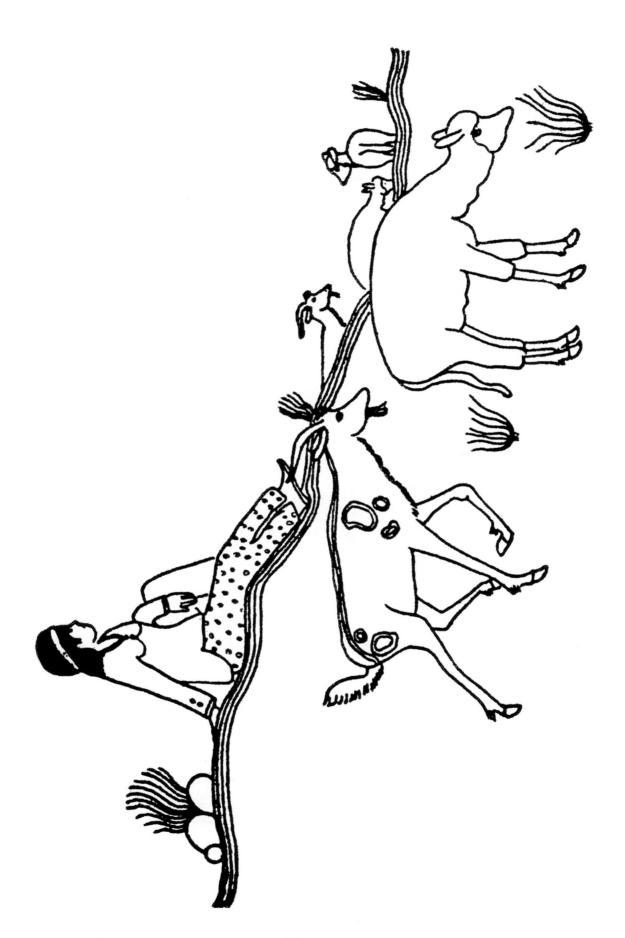

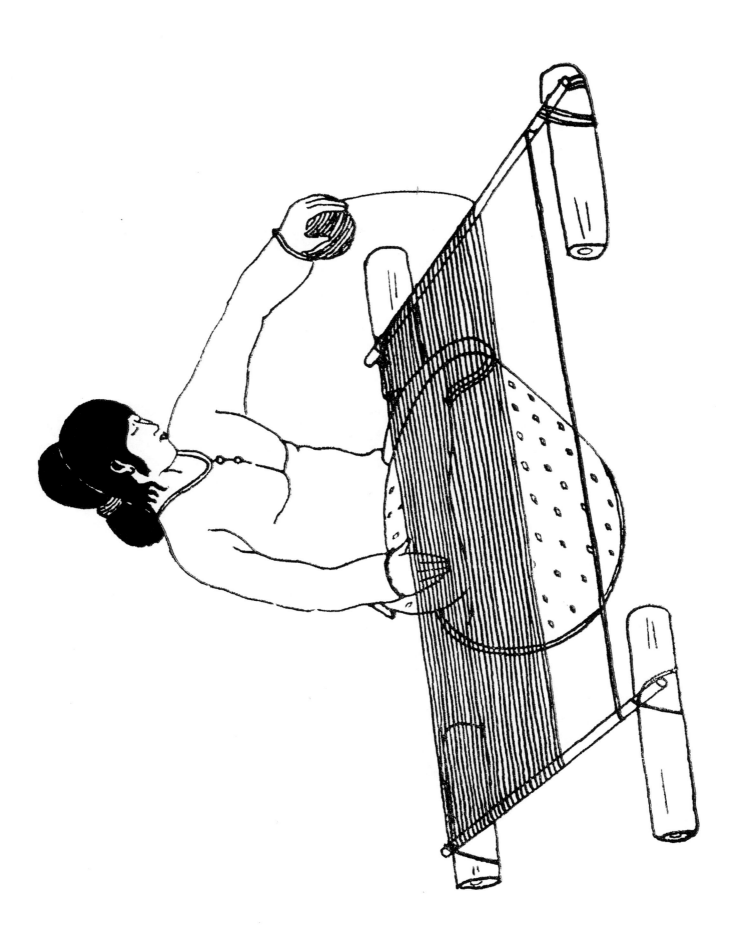